STOP ACCIDENTALLY MAKING THINGS WORSE

How to approach emotional outbursts:
Rewiring the brain to promote regulation, recovery and good decision making

A user friendly process to plan for and respond to individuals who cycle through intense behavior episodes

By: Josh Kuersten, M.Ed.

Who Am I?

First and foremost I am a parent of two beautiful children who are my greatest teachers. Each time I learn something through research, formal training or from my professional experience that I believe to be valuable, I bring it into my house and explore it with my children. They push my buttons, challenge my expectations, offer the most candid feedback and matter more to me than anyone else in my life. What I share with you here has the stamp of approval not only from thousands of hours of professional experience, but from years of testing and refining in my home and in my own life. The following information is not coming from the clinical world of carefully controlled office practice, but from the real world of messy unexpected circumstances with limited resources and diverse populations of individuals with differing beliefs and view points.

Professionally, I draw from over 25 years of experience working in education, specializing in special education with a focus on supporting students with behavior challenges and the staff members who work with them on a daily basis. I currently work as a behavior specialist in schools - teaching, training and coaching staff members how to best serve students whose behavior has overwhelmed everyone's local expertise. I believe my greatest gift in my work with schools comes from my breadth of experience, allowing me to have a deep understanding of the roles, politics and logistics that dominate school culture. Lessons learned from my days as a special day class paraprofessional and teacher, and through the opportunities that I have been given to teach behaviorally challenged students algebra, history, science and P.E in general education settings.

What follows is not the only way to do things, nor does it demand us giving up holding ourselves or others to high standards. This information challenges us to reorganize and reprioritize our actions, recognizing what is happening inside ourselves and others when experiencing stress and adjust our responses to match those needs. If I do my job well, you will gain a new perspective, bringing opportunity where there was once frustration and confusion.

Table of Contents

Foreword

None of us intentionally strive for conflict with children, nor do we enter into interaction trying to make things worse. With our best intentions, we try to make things right, to impart wisdom, skills and lessons, but so often we get it wrong. Our passion is so valuable as it leads us to action, yet so often pushes us off course as emotions arise and dictate the outcomes for both parties. Understanding the neurology of what is happening to a brain as it engages its emotional drive can help us to avoid these pitfalls, and get us, and the person that we are trying to support, out of the trap of the emotional mind.

Once we understand the landscape of the emotional mind, planning and implementing simple interventions that match what the brain needs, and is capable of responding to given its emotional state, will keep us away from contributing to the conflict at hand and help us move toward imparting true wisdom and coping skills to individuals in our care. These interactions are not only the most effective way to promote de-escalation in the moment, but offer the foundation on which tolerance is built, creating an environment that leads to true healing and long term change.

The Brain

Overview

- Brains are highly complex – built to recognize and solve problems; focused on helping individuals survive and thrive.
- The brain processes information sequentially, evaluating it through a specific set of neurological networks.
- The networks are prioritized based on their significance in relation to keeping us safe, healthy and alive.
- Networks are prioritized as follows: highest priority goes to those directly connected to bodily functions and sensory information, followed by emotional networks and finally critical thinking networks.
- The first two networks are closely linked as high priority networks – they directly inform, *and are highly influenced by*, our emotions.
- Our critical thinking, or "cognitive network" gets all of its information only after being filtered through our emotions, and is therefore only online and accessible during times of emotional baseline. This network is responsible for logically processing information, new learning, assessing multiple potential outcomes, impulse control and modulating emotions. Although a powerful problem solver, this network has the lowest priority for immediate survival and time intensive critical assessment, careful calculation and delays action in potentially harmful and / or life threatening situations.
- Understanding the sequential nature of our brains highlights the challenge we face as we interact with individuals under stress, as the human brain's ability to stay calm, control impulses, modulate emotional responses and act in a logical fashion is severely impaired during a stress response.

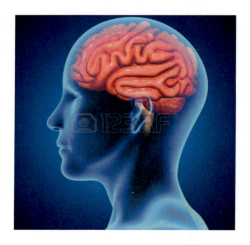

Dysregulation

Essentially, the human brain is "wired" to constantly monitor for, and respond to, potential threat signals before taking the time to engage in critical assessment that measures the potential outcome of one action over another. A basic review of Dr. Bruce Perry's work on the neurology of the stress response can help us understand how our brains operate when we are emotionally dysregulated.

Our brains process information in a sequential manner, giving higher priority of influence to messages that come from certain parts of our brain. Messages that light up neural networks responsible for survival, like those monitoring and adjusting for bodily functions and emotions like fear, have a stronger influence over how we respond to our environment than messages that are processed by parts of the brain dedicated to complex assessment, prediction, emotional modulation, new learning and complex problem solving and impulse control (Perry, 2013).

Helping us to stay alive and thrive, our survival networks focus on keeping the body running at peak efficiency by acting quickly in response to incoming information (often triggering and / or triggered by emotions). Rather than taking the time to pause and process information using critical assessment, running scenarios and predicting possible outcomes and effects on others before acting, our brain kicks us into quick action, supporting our primary directive to "survive and thrive." This "survival first" design is a double edge sword, serving us well in potentially harmful and life threatening situations where time is not a luxury, yet presenting a great challenge in emotionally escalated social situations. In these escalated social situations, our brain detects physical signs of escalation from our body (increased heart rate, breathing and changes in blood pressure), triggering emotions that perpetuate these signals, pushing us to respond with a bias toward survival. Once activated, this survival network essentially "switches off" our rational brain, blocking our ability to slow down and reflect, assess information rationally, measure our reactions against potential outcomes, mediate our impulsivity and modulate our response.

Healing

Trauma research suggests that brains exposed to chaotic patterns (especially environments where personal safety is chronically unpredictable) become "trained" to jump into survival mode more often, and in the face of smaller levels of stimuli, resulting in cycles of highly emotional responses that lead to chronic mental and physical health problems over time (Perry 2013, Harris, 2015). In addition to growing up in environments of chaos, individuals can also face temporary chronic stress when faced with specific life events that activate the stress response more easily, causing the brain to cycle through highly emotional responses. Examples of these external factors include financial, food, health, housing, relational and other environmental or personal challenges. Under these circumstances anyone can become sensitized, and individuals who already struggle with an over sensitive stress response will face even greater challenges and fall victim to emotional reactions to smaller levels of stimuli than normal (Perry, 2013).

Despite the harm that unpredictable and inconsistent environments have, the research also suggests that consistent / predictable patterns can heal. Exposure to environments that provide consistent and predictable patterns of stimuli can "rewire" the brain over time, helping to heal an overactive stress response and allow individuals to tolerate more and more challenges while maintaining emotional regulation (Perry, 2013). As healing begins to take hold, individuals rely less and less on their environment to support them and learn to self-regulate. Over time, self regulation builds increased tolerance, allowing individuals to stay in their "thinking brain" more often, modulating their emotions and maintaining impulse control in the face of life's ever changing circumstances.

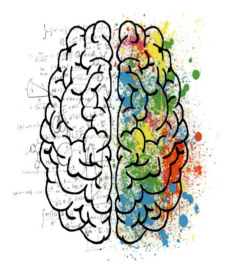

Review

Our brains are wired for survival. They are designed to prioritize physical and emotional signals that are out of the norm, demanding action to correct the problem. The brain is always monitoring internal and external signals, assessing needs and acting toward achieving physical and emotional regulation in an effort to support our primary directive to "survive and thrive."

A dysregulated brain is more sensitive and will respond to lower levels of discomfort with a heightened response. Once the stress response is triggered, the brain cannot slow down and assess the situation from multiple angles because the "thinking brain" shuts down to give priority to the networks that are responsible for responding quickly to keep us safe.

In unpredictable and inconsistent environments, our brains stress response goes into overdrive, becoming more and more sensitized, reacting in bigger and bigger ways to smaller stimulus. The only way to get out from under this overactive response is through exposure to consistent and predictable stimuli.

Understanding what the brain needs, we can move forward with a new framework, meeting individuals who demonstrate intense behavior with practices that promote regulation through carefully structured predictable and consistent responses. Whether planning for individuals who cycle through highly emotional responses, or facing an individual in the throws of a crisis, only a planned response that matches the needs of the individual's neurological state will begin to promote recovery, good decision making and essentially "rewire" the brain to respond in new and healthier ways.

This perspective is empowering, as **we** are the key to change. It is up to us to choose how we structure our environments and interact with individuals. We decide whether to provide predictability and consistency, and whether or not we respond to emotional individuals in ways that make things better or worse, both in the moment and over time…

The Process

- Observation
- Reflection
- Planning
- Implementation

Given this framework, how do we "rewire" brains, to promote regulation, recovery, and good decision making? The worksheet in this book is designed specifically to allow anyone to guide themselves through the observation, planning and implementation of effective strategies for any individual, creating an environment rich with predictability and consistency, directing responses that match the neurological states of the individuals that we are working with.

The most effective way to use this resource is to choose a specific individual that cycles through intense behavior, and work through each step of this book with that person in mind. The following pages will walk you through a visual representation of the stress response cycle, illustrating an individual's changing brain as they move outside of their emotional baseline, through escalation and crisis, into recovery and back to baseline. At each stage of the process, observation, reflection, planning and implementation will be discussed as you fill in specific steps to take with your target individual, ending in a working document that will guide the structure of your environment and your interactions, helping to bring healing through consistency and predictability.

Please refer to your included worksheet for the rest of the book

This worksheet can be found on the final page of this ebook.

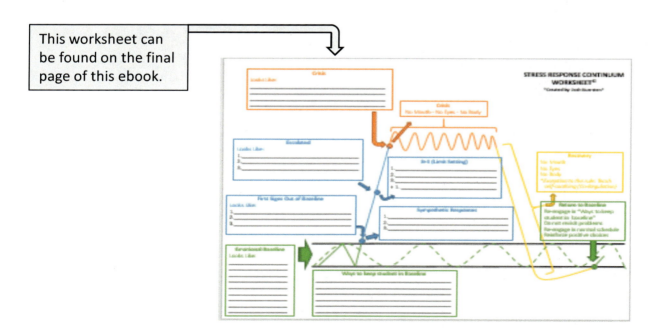

Baseline

Baseline

The illustration below correlates to the image at the bottom of your worksheet. It represents emotional regulation. The top and bottom borders of this "emotional baseline" represent the highs and lows of each individual's "normal," while the green waves represent typical emotional swings within their "normal" range. Normal is in quotes, because each person has their own range of "normal," some having a greater range of highs and lows than others. This area fluctuates in size depending on the level of self-regulation that an individual has developed and the circumstances that they are currently experiencing in their lives. It is important to note that each individual is different, that our "normal" is not the same as anyone else's, that each of us can be loud or quiet, excited or subdued, alert or inattentive at a level that still falls within our "normal" range, and that depending on life's circumstances, what was "normal" one day may not be the next.

Most importantly, baseline represents the **ONLY** time that any individual has access to their full cognitive potential. This represents our brain before the initiation of a stress response, before our "thinking brain" begins to go offline. **This is the ONLY time that we can learn new things, be patient, listen and fully process information, problem solve, and modulate our emotions, impulsivity and reactions to our internal and external environment.**

This means that our most important job in supporting individuals in our care is to help maintain this norm, or return them to this norm before we expect them to move on with any part of their day, calm down, connect their actions to outcomes, accept consequences, resolve conflict or engage in learning activities.

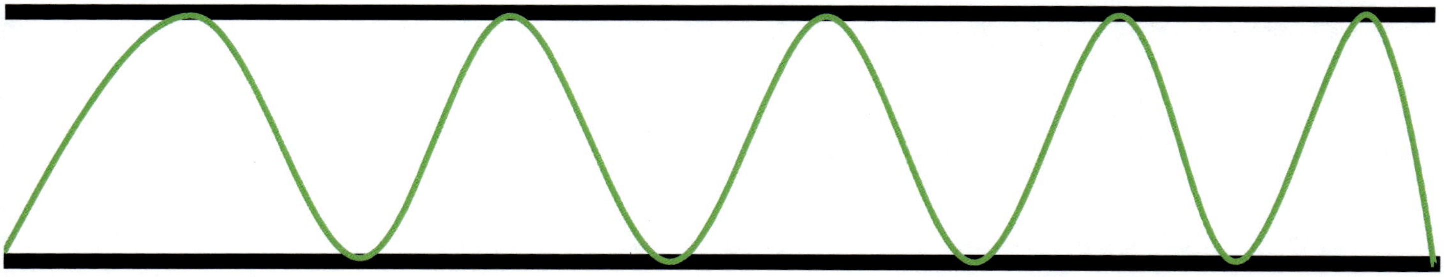

Baseline

Expecting an individual to move on to their next responsibility, to the next part of the project, to the next thing on their schedule, to let go of a problem, to follow through with a direction, etc..., means **first** assuring that they are already in baseline or supporting them in returning to baseline. It will only serve to escalate an individual if they are pushed through situations when they are dysregulated.

Individuals can still be expected to follow through with their responsibilities, be held to high standards and accept consequences for their actions, but only when emotionally regulated. The alternative is to have their escalated behavior trump any demands or expectations being placed on them which promotes reinforcing the very behavior that we wish to change. Remember, dysregulation is a brain state that cannot simply be turned off. We must support individuals in bringing their "thinking brain" back online before we can expect them to learn how to handle things more appropriately. If they are not in a place where their brain can take in new information, our efforts will only serve to escalate the situation.

For educators, this is powerful because it redefines our priorities. If the only time any new learning can happen is when a person is inside their baseline, and the purpose of school is to learn, then getting into and keeping individuals in their baseline **now becomes 100% of our job**. This means adjusting our priorities and ensuring that we support individuals in moving to or maintaining baseline before leading them through any activities. This same priority easily translates to parent, child, partner and adult interaction in our daily lives.

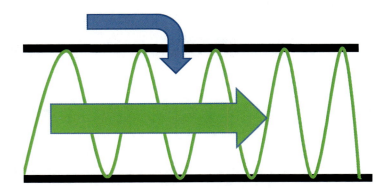

Baseline

Using the worksheet, first identify what baseline looks like for your target individual. This is something that we learn over time. The first day you meet someone, you do your best to assess their emotional state based on social norms and past experience; you have no idea where they are within the highs and lows of their unique baseline. However, over time, you can get to know someone pretty well. The best way to understand how to know when your target individual is in baseline or not is to imagine your target individual and think to yourself what it is like when they walk through the door and you think to yourself, "ah, this is going to be a good morning!" versus "I want to get away from this person right now!"

ACTIVITY: **Part 1** – Picture your target individual and reflect on what informs your intuition that they are inside emotional baseline instead of out. Pick out 3 concrete, observable behaviors that you can identify as happening when things are going right, and write these things into the "Emotional Baseline Looks Like" box. An example of this may be: Greets adults with eye contact, will readily converse about dinosaurs, is easily verbally redirected. In some individuals this can look like: body always moving, socializing with peers, lots of hands on play (both individuals smiling and laughing), responds to touch on shoulder for gaining attention, engages in routines independently.

These are things that you would expect to see when your target individual is emotionally regulated, and would not expect to see when they are not.

Emotional Baseline Looks Like:

_____

_____

_____

_____

_____

_____

Ways to keep student in Baseline

_____

_____

_____

_____

9

Baseline

The information on what baseline looks like is critical for many reasons. First, this is how you know if your target individual is ready to participate in daily activities as opposed to needing to be supported in regulation before starting. Secondly, this is our common language among the adults and other support people in this individual's environment. It is how to communicate to others what to look for in this individual to assess if they are regulated or not. Finally, this information is what will guide us as we assess readiness after an episode of dysregulation. This is so important because if we try to engage too early after an individual's escalated episode, we will actually push the individual back into escalation. This becomes increasingly challenging the further outside of baseline a child becomes.

ACTIVITY: **Part 2** – Now that you have documented what it looks like when your target individual is in baseline, it's time to identify what it is that supports keeping them there. Consider what you put into the "looks like" box, their personality type, their learning style, social skills, movement needs, strengths and weaknesses, and the resources available to you. Taking all of this into consideration, write down 3 things in the "Ways to keep in baseline" box that you can provide to help keep this individual inside of baseline when they are already there. This may look like: minimal verbal interaction when highly focused, timers for transitions, strict routines to support non-preferred activities, consistent check in and close proximity from adults, etc… .

Emotional Baseline
Looks Like:

_____

_____

_____

_____

_____

_____

Ways to keep student in Baseline

_____

_____

_____

_____

Review

   Baseline is the only time that an individual has access to their full cognitive potential. The emotional networks are quiet and the capacity to fully process incoming information, modulate emotions, exert impulse control and understand how present choices affect future outcomes is accessible.

   Baseline is out target focus, adjusting the environment and implementing strategies for interaction that support keeping an individual in their baseline or helping to move them back to their baseline. Expecting an individual to move on to their next responsibility, to the next part of the project, to the next thing on their schedule, to let go of a problem, to follow through with a direction, etc..., means **first** assuring that they are already in baseline or supporting them in returning to baseline. It will only serve to escalate an individual if they are pushed through situations when they are dysregulated.

   The most productive use of our time is to work with individuals in ways that help them sustain emotional baseline. It is from this state that we can move individuals into new learning, expose them to challenges, and increase their tolerance, helping them to be better prepared for the myriad of variables that life will throw into their path.

Triggered
On the Precipice

Triggered
On the Precipice

Just as the previous area of focus, baseline, is arguably the most important place to put our efforts as it helps to plan for and keep individuals regulated, this next area of focus is possibly the most important as we begin to discuss *intervention*. I think of this stage as "being on the precipice" because after this everything starts to go downhill. Escalation past this point, takes **BOTH** the target individual **AND** the support person for a ride (along with anyone else in the environment). Unless we are keenly aware and responsive, escalation will occur and gain a life of its own as additional individuals become dysregulated, creating a multiplication of variables that contribute to furthering emotional escalation.

Adding to the significance of this stage of the stress response cycle is the recognition that **this is the last time that we are dealing with a "thinking brain."** This is our last opportunity to be supportive, negotiate alternatives and avoid extended time for recovery.

Our work at this stage is to identify what it looks like when an individual becomes triggered. In a moment, reflect on this individual and identify the first signs of dysregulation writing them into the box labeled "First Signs Out of Baseline." These behaviors signal that the individual is on the precipice of emotional escalation and if things keep going, they will go over the edge soon. It is imperative that we identify these early signs and put the bulk of our **intervention** efforts here, as the process is inherently "messy" after this point.

First Signs Out of Baseline
Looks Like:
1._____
2._____
3._____

Sympathetic Responses
1._____
2._____
3._____

Triggered
On the Precipice

The two major points to remember here are:

1. This is the last time that you are dealing with a "logical" individual. Negotiation, cause and effect, delayed gratification and rational communication are still an option. From a rational standpoint, this is why things get messy beyond this point. As things escalate further, both the individual and the support provider's ability to communicate, problem solve and regulate become compromised, so even carefully planned and well executed intervention is potentially messy.

2. This is the last time that you do not have to account for an extended recovery period before emotional baseline is regained. As the "thinking brain" is still online, appropriate support allows an individual to slip right back into regulation without having to "reboot" their cognitive network. From a scheduling standpoint, this takes much less time and energy, allowing everyone to stay on schedule with minimal interruption.

When an individual is triggered, the brain has identified "something is off" but has not yet begun the cascade of neurochemistry that fires up the defenses and initiates dysregulation. Channels of communication are still open, and if we can offer appropriate support, the individual should slide right back into baseline. This is not only a time saver, but it avoids the potential to send us and others into an escalated state, so often creating an emotional and logistical nightmare that, if repeated regularly, leads to an environment that breeds anxiety, stress and eventual trauma that can have long lasting negative effects (Harris, 2015).

First Signs Out of Baseline
Looks Like:
1._____
2._____
3._____

Sympathetic Responses
1._____
2._____
3._____

Triggered
On the Precipice

ACTIVITY: **Part 1** – Identify what it looks like when your target individual first starts to show signs of "out of baseline" and write them into the corresponding box on your worksheet. Some examples are: not engaged with materials, looking around / scanning the environment, turning toward others to initiate engagement, small noises, clenched fists, sighs and a head drop, blurting out, stomping, increased distractibility, delayed response (mild ignoring), whining or other changes of vocal tone etc… .

The key here is to try and identify the very first signals that alert us to a potential escalation. I've noticed in live training that often when doing this reflection activity, people usually come up with the second or third sign that signals an individual is being triggered, but when going back and observing, they find one or two earlier clues to potential escalation. This information is so valuable because once identified, supportive adults can interrupt their normal flow to offer immediate support without missing a beat and move the individual right back into baseline, avoiding escalation all together. Even when immersed in responsibility, noticing one of the signs can signal adults to stop what they are doing and offer immediate intervention.

Part 2 – Once you have written down the signs that put you on notice for a potential escalation, it is time to move to the box labeled "Sympathetic Responses" and write down three strategies that you can use to help your target individual return to baseline. These often include typical strategies like proximity, offers of help, changing materials, changing location, engaging in rational negotiation, asking engaging questions, etc… .

First Signs Out of Baseline
Looks Like:
1._____
2._____
3._____

Sympathetic Responses
1._____
2._____
3._____

Triggered
On the Precipice

At this point in the process you have the bulk of the information you need to operate in the most productive part of the process. Brains that are regulated can engage, and engaged brains do not easily dysregulate. When you are moving through your day and notice your target individual exhibiting one the signs that you have documented, the most productive action you can take is to respond with one or more of your sympathetic responses. If the individual moves back into regulation, you are good to go; if not, you will simply abandon "sympathetic" responses and move to the next phase of intervention.

As a matter of practice, once you are in this mindset, continue to reflect on your daily experience and adjust your notes to further specificity in relation to early signs of potential escalation and the sympathetic responses that are the most effective. Keeping yourself mindful will help you to develop powerfully effective interventions and allow you to keep up with the developmental changes of the individual that you are supporting.

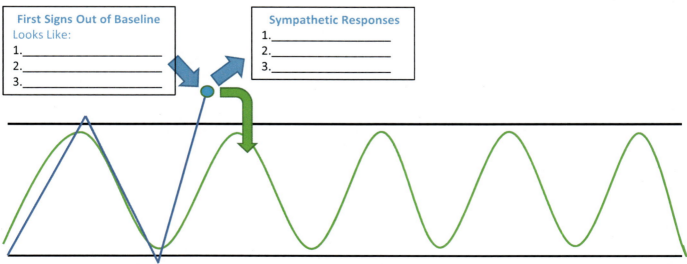

First Signs Out of Baseline
Looks Like:
1._____
2._____
3._____

Sympathetic Responses
1._____
2._____
3._____

Review

When an individual is triggered, **it is the last time that we are dealing with a regulated individual.** The "thinking brain" is still accessible, but the emotional networks are beginning to ramp up. In terms of intervention, this is the most effective place for care providers to step in. This is the last opportunity to be supportive, negotiate alternatives and avoid extended time for recovery. Past this point, intervention is inherently messy.

Support looks like sympathetic responses and can include offers of help, assistance in finding space to be alone, engaging in alternative activities, adding or removing proximity, rescheduling tasks, switching the medium of receptive and / or expressive communication, interaction that engages highly motivating subject matter etc... . This is a major turning point in the process. If the individual is able to resume baseline regulation, then move on with typical planned support to help them maintain baseline. If the individual continues to escalate, we must switch how we approach support as the brain no longer reacts well to sympathetic responses, and approaching individuals in this manner will only make things worse.

Escalation

Escalation

Escalation can occur when we miss the early signals an individual displays, or when we do respond to a triggered individual and the support we offer is not enough to interrupt the brain's emotional response.

The important thing to note here is that intervention strategies that work for a triggered individual DO NOT WORK for an escalated individual. Trying to be supportive at this stage will only serve to further escalate an individual. It is important to remember that once an individual hits escalation, their neurology shifts, and their reality changes. They no longer have the capacity to problem solve, negotiate, analyze, or consider how their "now" actions affect their "future" choices.

At this point, individuals are living in the present and need a clear set of limited choices that fulfill an immediate need. To deliver these choices effectively, we must use what I refer to as minimal effective interaction (as few words as possible, short duration of proximity and non-emotional tone of voice followed by removal of close proximity, eye contact and verbal interaction immediately after limits are communicated).

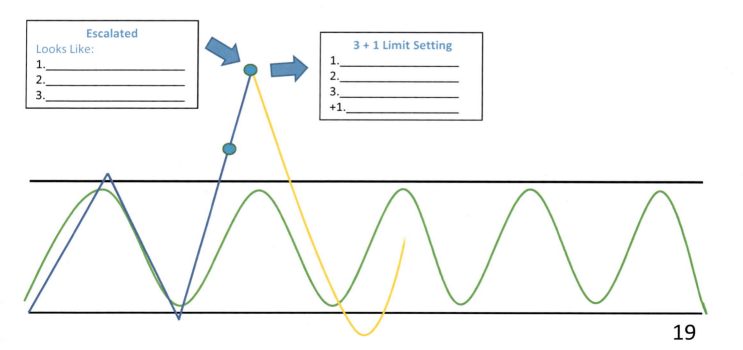

Escalation

It is important to recognize that this is the part of the process that can look "messy." Our brains are wired for socialization, utilizing mirror neurons to mimic others responses and help us feel what they are feeling in order to effectively communicate. Although supportive in healthy interaction, our own neurology begins to promote dysregulation when supporting individuals in this state. Having a clear understanding of limits and communication strategies before finding ourselves in this situation is paramount to our ability to engage without contributing to the problem.

Being emotional beings, this is the stage where supportive adults typically struggle the most, creating problems that didn't exist because in the process of helping, we are triggered by the present circumstances. It is our own stress response that misinforms us and adds chaos to the moment. The most effective way to counteract this is to be very clear about what it looks like when an individual is escalated, where our limits are, and exactly what it looks like to communicate those limits. If done correctly, you will be giving this person (and yourself) the best chance to avoid total dysregulation (crisis / tantrum / melt-down... it is known as many names) and return to a regulated state.

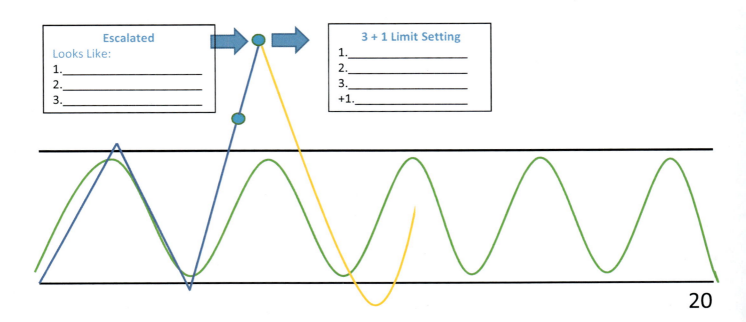

Escalation

Additionally, this is the first time in the process where we must recognize that an individual will need additional recovery time (for their neurology to reset). This is noted in yellow on the illustration below. This represents a process that follows escalation, and demands our patience while the brain resets before we see regulated behavior again. Attempting to engage an individual before they have had a chance to recover will send them back into escalation and start the process all over again.

ACTIVITY: **Part 1** – Identify what it looks like when the individual that you are focusing on first starts to show signs of escalation and write them in the box labeled "Escalated." This is a higher intensity than being triggered, and may look like: getting up, wandering, repeated attempts to verbally engage or disrupt, getting into other's personal space or off limit areas, ignoring directions, walking away from supervising adults, use of inappropriate language, making derogatory comments about others, increased volume – tone – cadence of voice, posturing, talking over others etc... .

The key here is to identify what escalation looks like for this specific individual. These are signs that the emotional brain is taking over and signals us to change our intervention from interaction that offers multiple options and negotiation to a minimal effective interaction approach aimed at meeting the immediate needs of the individual.

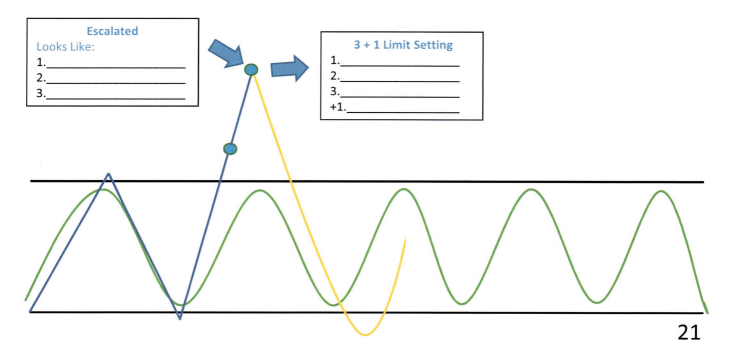

Escalated
Looks Like:
1._____
2._____
3._____

3 + 1 Limit Setting
1._____
2._____
3._____
+1._____

Escalation

ACTIVITY: **Part 2** – As soon as we see any of the "Escalated" behaviors documented on our worksheet, we must move directly to minimal effective interaction, and offer clear choices that are acceptable to us and offer an immediate alternative for the escalated individual. Document these choices in the box labeled "3 + 1 Limit Setting." The "3 + 1" format creates a clear and simple set of choices designed to disrupt the escalation cycle by altering incoming stimulus and helping individuals engage in regulating and / or rewarding activities.

In "3+1 limit setting," the first 3 choices are options that support self regulation and can be generalized to many situations and environments, engaging the individual in simple activities that remove demands and the need for social interaction. In most environments, these choices tend to be reading, drawing or resting (during which time, no verbal interaction with others is allowed) and can be accessed right in their current space, or in a pre-determined alternative location.

Considering your environment, and your target individual, use the worksheet to write down 3 choices that support simple ways to disconnect from demands and engage in activities that are easily generalized and support self-regulation. Remember, we are structuring predictability and consistency in order to re-wire brains, so the intervention choices at this step cannot be contingent. All choices must be immediate options, accessible to all individuals, even when escalated behavior is being exhibited.

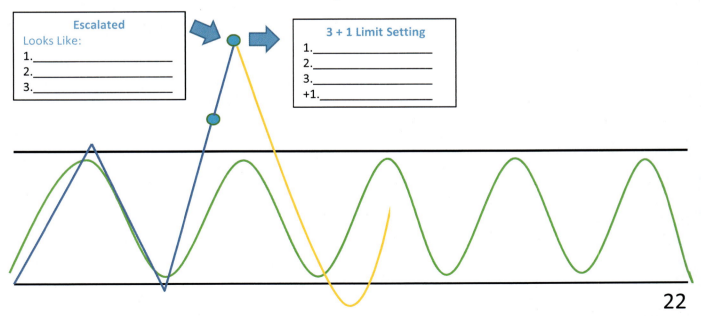

Escalation

Identifying 3 win / win choices before a problem occurs puts us in a much better position to act from a minimal effective interaction standpoint because chances are good that when supporting escalated individuals, WE are also becoming escalated, forcing our critical thinking brains to become compromised. Pre-planning becomes imperative to our success at this stage as "thinking on our feet" usually leads to extended interaction, increased emotional reaction and only serves to escalate both the individual that we are supporting and ourselves.

In addition to three general choices, some individuals require an additional level of support. These "+ 1" choices are typically a co-regulation option that involves supporting individuals who do not yet have the capacity to self regulate by participating in the three general choices, and / or a functional option that meets the need motivating their negative behavior in a more socially acceptable way. These options usually place increased time and resource demands on those in support roles, but serve to help individuals in the long run as co-regulation is a pre-requisite to learning self-regulation, helping individuals to meet their needs independently over time.

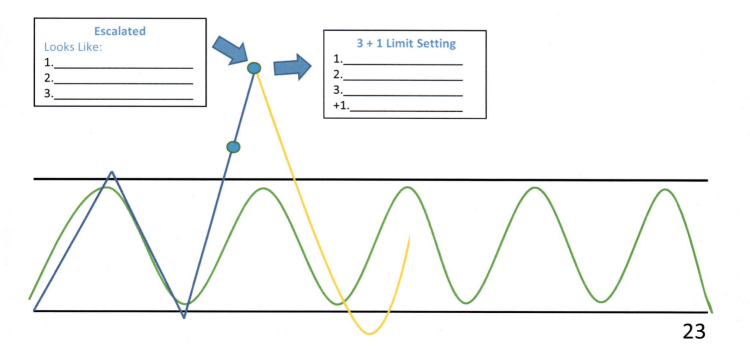

Escalated
Looks Like:
1._____
2._____
3._____

3 + 1 Limit Setting
1._____
2._____
3._____
+1._____

Escalation

Consider the individual you are planning for and look at the 3 general choices that you already have. Ask yourself if these options are realistic when this person is escalated? The example choices (read, draw, rest) all demand the ability to maintain a specific activity without interacting with others. If this is not what your person needs, then consider adding a "+ 1" choice that allows the individual access to co-regulation choices such as going on a walk with a support person or accessing special activities including access to typically off limit locations, signing onto computers or playing basketball with a supportive individual. Also consider physical and social needs. Does this person need movement? Are they driven by social interaction, screen time or crave adult attention? Weigh these needs against what you can consistently offer based on logistics and resources and write down a "+ 1" that you can dependably offer every time.

Pre-planning and pre-teaching clear and simple choices allow adults to respond effectively in the moment by simply by saying, "I need you to use your choices before I can _____." This type of response not only supports minimal effective interaction, it also allows adults to easily enforce limits as the contingency to follow directions is about what **the adults** will do instead of placing further demands on the individual that force the adult into a disempowered position as they wait for an appropriate response, often leading to their own escalation and attempts toward further levels of punitive action that fuels increased escalated behavior.

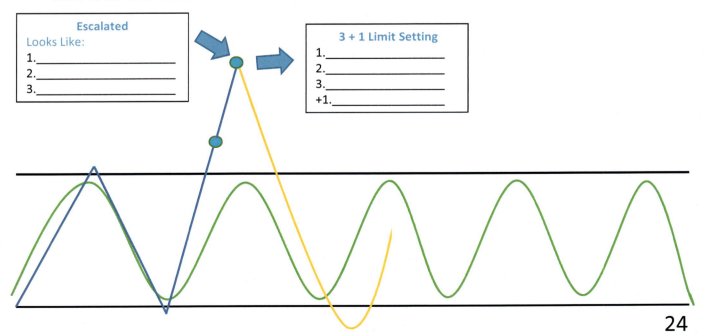

Escalation

This response also supports consistency and predictability as all adults supporting this individual can give the same direction under the same circumstances time and time again. The 3 + 1 model is so valuable in that the three general choices are most often offered to all individuals in an environment, where as the + 1 choices is only given to those who need that extra level of support. In this way, multiple adults do not have to keep lists of choices clear in their head, they just need to know the general choices and a few individualized options for those who need that extra layer of support.

Based on the needs of the individuals in your care, choices can be written down and / or visually represented to further support communication, especially during times of escalation when cognitive abilities are already compromised. In many environments these choices are posted on a wall, on desks, in folders, or in designated break locations. Posted choices help support adults as well as individuals needing support as escalation tends to challenge everyone's ability to communicate clearly.

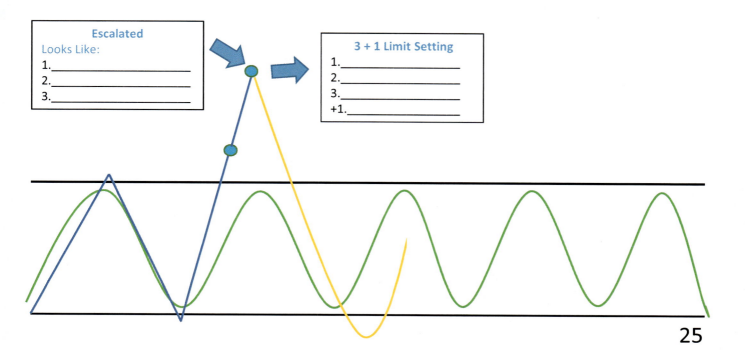

Review

Escalation means that the brain is now in a dysregulated state. Expect to see behaviors like demanding, defiance, ignoring, threatening, and verbal lashing out. At this stage, individuals are not able to modulate their emotions appropriately, show impulse control, adjust their current actions under threat of later consequences, negotiate alternatives or accept sympathetic support from others.

Cognition is now compromised and the "thinking brain" is offline. In order to intervene effectively, care providers must reduce their responses to minimal effective interaction. Immediacy is the key. "Now" choices need to yield "now" outcomes. The best intervention offers a set of consistent choices using consistent language, creating a predictable pattern for the brain to recognize over time. It does not guarantee that the escalation will stop immediately, but it does have the highest probability of doing so; and it is exactly what needs to happen to create the pattern of consistency that leads to healing over time.

Equally important is the recognition that care providers are typically pulled outside of baseline concurrently in the presence of escalation and their cognition also suffers. Pre-planned choices, and scripts that ensure minimal effective interaction offer the best potential for care providers to avoid accidentally escalating the situation further. Additionally, having carefully planned responses has the effect of reducing stress and allows care providers to remain more regulated, even in the face of other peoples stress response.

Crisis Response

Crisis Response

When we see an individual experiencing a crisis response, we are witnessing the full effect of "fight or flight." The "logical brain" is no longer online. Our interaction needs to be clean and clear to avoid adding to the intensity or duration of their response. The rules of interaction are simple, but putting them into action is challenging. Simply put, it is through the **removal** of interaction, not through engagement, that we can offer the greatest support to any individual experiencing this level of stress response. Verbal interaction, eye contact, and proximity enter a dysregulated brain as additional sensory input into an already overwhelmed environment. Placing greater processing demand on individuals during crisis only adds to the chaos and serves to escalate them further. It is mandatory that we disengage at this time. If we must act, it should only be to address others in the environment, helping create as much space as we can for the individual in crisis and allowing them all the time they need to recover.

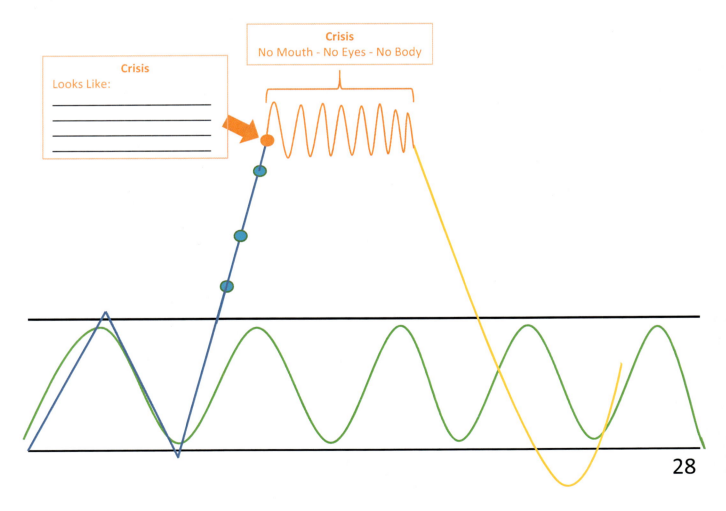

28

Crisis Response

It is very difficult for most people to disengage at this point. Typically the behavior being exhibited by an individual at this stage of escalation is crossing all kinds of acceptable boundaries, pushing care providers into their own escalation. As both individuals escalate, it creates a group dynamic fueling an environment of emotional responses that feed each other. As each individual's actions and reactions continue trigger one another, they push each other further and further into crisis. It is like a psychological wild fire that creates it's own weather, further fanning the flames of neuro-emotional hijacking.

The struggle we face in changing our response to this situation is that all of this is a result of typical neurology. It is what our brain is designed to do. We are hard wired to respond with strong emotions to a severe imbalance in the environment, triggering a swift response in an attempt to correct the problem.

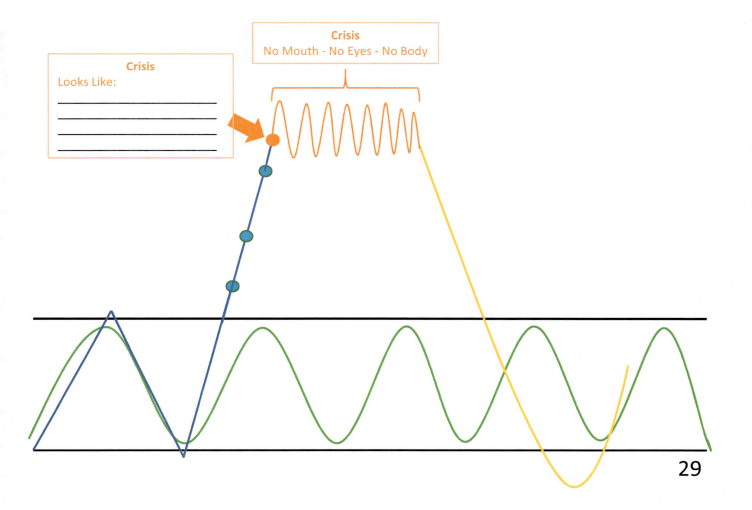

Crisis Response

This is where our own journey of self regulation begins. Not only does creating predictability and consistency through our interactions with individuals create healing and promote tolerance for them, it does the same for us. As we dedicate ourselves to following the 3 simple rules of responding to someone in crisis – NO MOUTH, NO EYES, NO BODY – we begin to "rewire" our own neurology and combat the knee jerk emotional responses that feed the fire of crisis.

By defining crisis (In the "Crisis Looks Like:" box on the worksheet), we create predictability for ourselves and those in our care, offering a consistent point at which we shift away from interaction and move to honoring an individual's time and space, supporting their journey back to baseline. By creating these definable points along the stress response continuum, we reduce our own anxiety around "what to do when," and offer a predictable and consistent pattern of response that supports an environment of healing and tolerance for everyone.

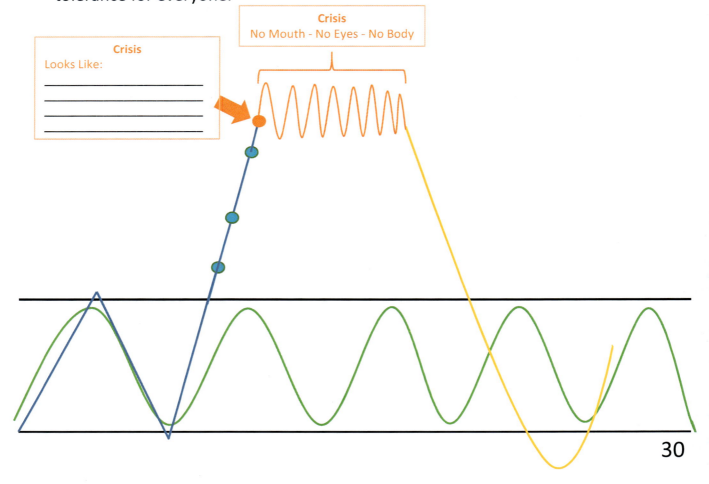

Crisis Response

Breaking down the rules of interaction: no eyes, no mouth, no body. Remember that at this point in the stress response cycle, an individual's brain is now overloaded with emotions and is seeking immediate relief. Their logical brain is completely offline and they are not able to process incoming information in healthy or productive ways. The most effective way to offer intervention at this point is to reduce as much input as possible. The best way to do this is stop talking, break eye contact and move away.

I can't say enough about the first rule – no mouth – stop talking. This is the one rule that I see over and over again undercut intervention and consistently make problems worse. When you talk to a person in crisis, you are speaking to someone who is illogical. By definition, their cognitive brain is offline, so they cannot make connections to action and consequence, alternative solutions, negotiation, problem solving or emotional modulation. Your words only serve to prolong the crisis and increase the intensity of their response.

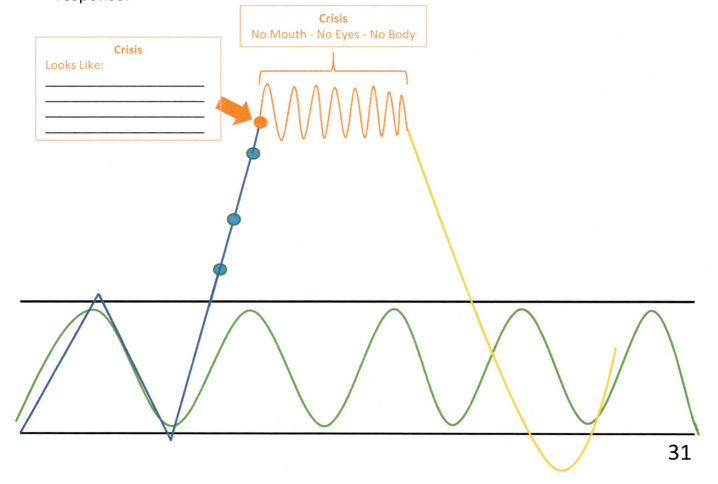

Crisis Response

This means that saying "no hitting" when someone is hitting, or "no throwing" when someone is throwing things actually makes the problem worse. I am not saying that no hitting or no throwing should not be a rule, that it should not have consequences, or that you should somehow allow hitting and throwing. What I am saying is that talking about hitting, throwing, or any other behavior in the midst of a crisis response is not going to do anything except promote the very behavior that you wish to stop. The time to discuss behavior expectations and consequences is when the logical brain is ready to listen, during times of baseline. If you think about it, the only time a person is ever going to follow through with a consequence is when they are under emotional control anyway, so don't waste your time and don't make things worse in the moment; allow the person time and space to recover and deal with the situation once everyone is at baseline once again.

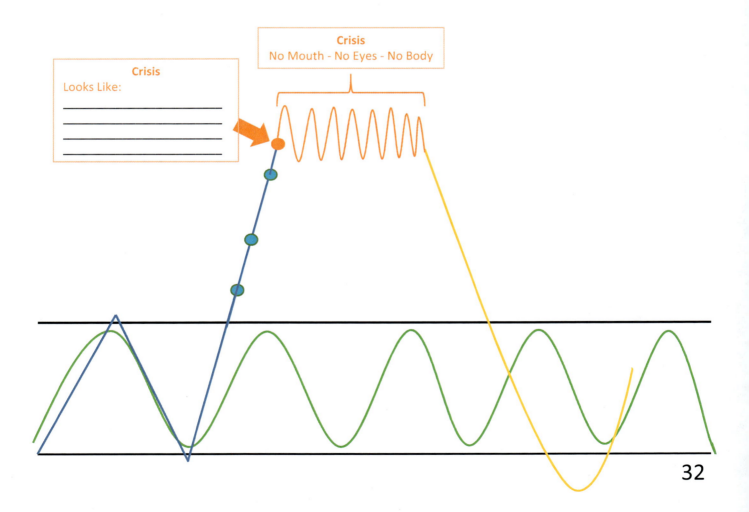

Crisis Response

In the same way that verbal interaction just comes in as noise that adds to the chaos of a brain in crisis, eye contact and proximity do the same. Supervision can happen without eye contact, and because you are not talking to a person, you do not need to seek feedback from their facial expressions. You can use your peripheral vision or look at someone's feet to keep track of where they are and assess if their body language clues you in to a potential shift toward recovery. Additionally, proximity can be a huge trigger for most people in crisis as the presence of another person places an unspoken demand on an individual, inferring "I'm going to wait here until you change your behavior, and it needs to happen on my timeline, not yours." Moving away and shifting your body position so that you are facing slightly away from the person is the most effective way to present yourself physically during a person's crisis response. Additionally, engaging in something other than "waiting for the behavior to change" will add to the effectiveness of your intervention. Easy tricks include engaging with others or checking email on your phone.

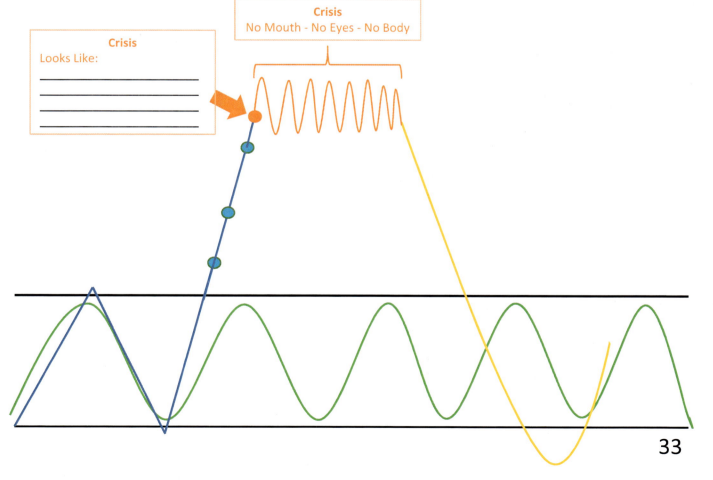

Crisis Response

If there are others in the environment, the best thing that you can do is engage with them and help support them to honor the space and time of the person in crisis. Be transparent about what is happening and help them to respond in a caring and respectful manner toward the escalated individual by offering zero verbal interaction, eye contact or proximity until they are back under emotional control. Engaging with others helps direct the emotional energy that is created by the situation and offers reinforcement of a safe, predictable and consistent environment for the person in crisis and everyone else who is involved in, or witness to the situation.

ACTIVITY: Identify what a crisis response looks like for your target individual and write it into the "Crisis Looks Like" box on the worksheet. Describe the behavior that tells you they are unlikely to process anything you say, triggering a no mouth, no eyes, no body response from you. Anytime this behavior is present, all adults shift their response away from all interaction, supporting a predictable and consistent environment.

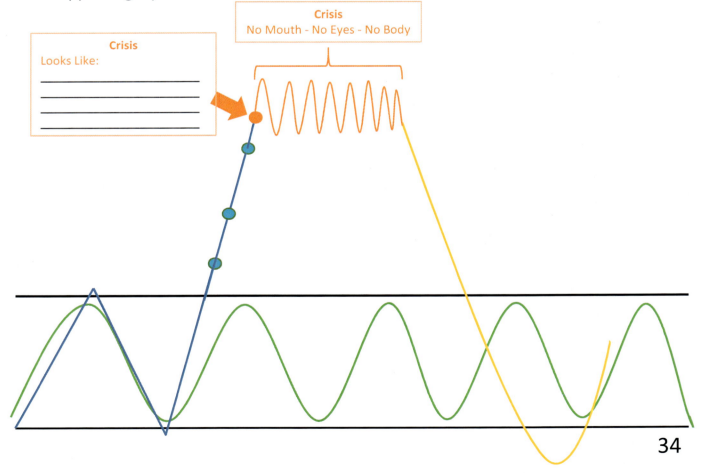

Review

A crisis Response is full blown fight or flight. The "thinking brain" is not accessible as the sensory and emotional networks are now flooding the brain with information. Any attempt to interact with an individual experiencing a crisis response is likely to make things worse and last longer. The best response is a carefully planned non-response. Care providers must disengage all verbal interaction, break eye contact and move away from the individual. Energy should be channeled into creating space and time for the individual. Remove others and engage in proactive choices that structure a safe and supportive environment for recovery post crisis.

Recognize that as a care provider, you will most likely be highly escalated at this point as well. Following the simple set of rules: no mouth – no eyes – no body offers the best potential to mitigate the intensity and duration of the crisis, and eliminates demand for decision making in times of impaired judgement. Both care providers and individuals in their care need time and space to move through this stage of the stress response.

Recovery

Recovery

So often missed, and one of the most important areas of the stress response cycle, is recovery. Recovery is the time between escalated behavior and an individual's return to baseline. It is represented by the yellow line on the worksheet. Individuals need recovery anytime they escalate past the "triggered" phase of the stress response cycle, as their neurology has shifted toward fight or flight and needs time to reset, allowing the "thinking brain" to come back online.

A common mistake people make is trying to interact with an individual prematurely, placing demands on individuals who have not fully recovered from escalated emotional states, inadvertently sending them back into escalation.

Recovery often takes a lot of time and patience. The rules of responding to crisis also apply to recovery: no mouth, no eyes, no body. Supporting recovery means waiting until baseline behavior is present again. This can be tricky because we are often still escalated ourselves and our judgement of other's emotional state is impaired. Thankfully we have the worksheet to rely on. Our first exercise was to write down what baseline looks like for our target person, and it is those signs that tell us when to interact once again.

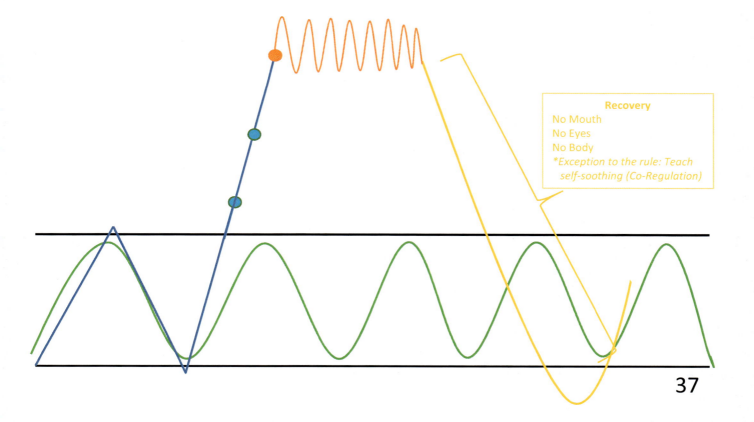

Recovery
No Mouth
No Eyes
No Body
*Exception to the rule: Teach
 self-soothing (Co-Regulation)

Recovery

We must check any of our own desires to move on, or attempts by the individual to engage that do not match what is in the "Emotional Baseline looks like" box, before we re-engage with an individual. If we do not see baseline behavior, we continue to disengage and wait.

A common mistake people make is trying to interact with an individual prematurely. Placing demands on individuals who have not fully recovered from escalated emotional states, inadvertently send them back into escalation. One of the most difficult phases of the recovery cycle to assess happens just before return to baseline where an individual experiences a depression of sorts (circled in yellow below). This often appears as very subdued behavior, sleepiness, boredom or even exquisite compliance. Following an escalated incident, all of these behaviors can be very inviting as "the worst of it" is over and can trick us into premature interaction. If we fall into this trap, we risk pushing individuals back into escalated or crisis behavior. Again, we must check the behavior and ask ourselves, "is this typical baseline behavior?" Does this person usually present themselves as this compliant, this tired or this subdued?" If the answer is no, then continue to disengage until baseline behavior returns.

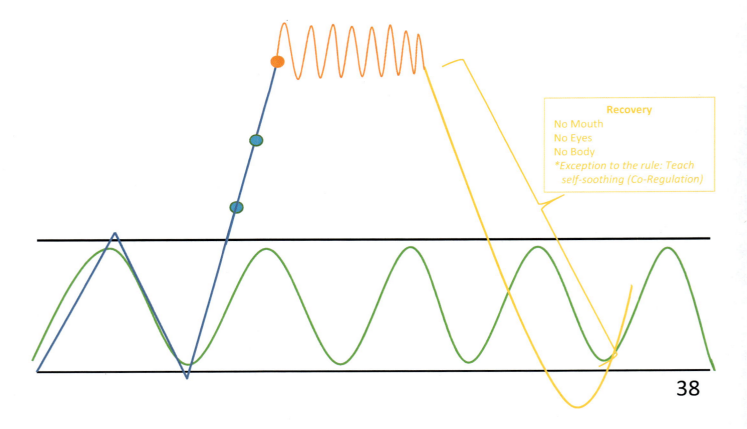

Recovery
No Mouth
No Eyes
No Body
*Exception to the rule: Teach self-soothing (Co-Regulation)

Recovery

The exception to the rule: There is an exception to the rule of total disengagement through the entire recovery cycle. This happens when an individual consistently cycles back into crisis over and over again regardless of the removal of verbal interaction, eye contact and proximity. If this pattern is observed over time (not just during one incident, but each time the individual escalates they seem to be unable to recover regardless of the time and space given to them), then it is most likely because they do not have the skills or the practice in using the skills to self regulate. This means that careful planning needs to take place in order to identify what part of recovery is optimal for interaction, and exactly what can be done by outside individuals to promote co-regulation (a pre-requisite to self-regulation). Co-regulation will often already be identified as a + 1 choice on the worksheet. Like all other areas of intervention, co-regulation needs to be well defined. A predictable line must be established for when outside interaction is attempted, what is said and done, what constitutes continued interaction and where the line of repeated disengagement is if the individual does not respond productively.

An example might be: When Billy is no longer physically acting out prompt once, "want to take a walk with me?" If Billy responds with threatening language or posturing, disengage all verbal interaction, eye contact and proximity. If Billy offers any verbal signal of acceptance, do not make eye contact, say, "I'll wait for you at the door," and wait for Billy to join.

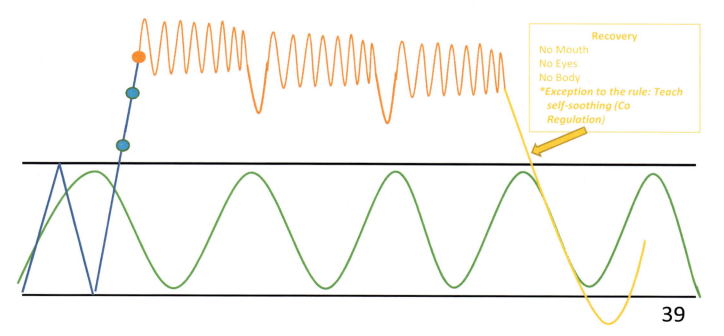

Recovery
No Mouth
No Eyes
No Body
*Exception to the rule: Teach self-soothing (Co Regulation)

Review

Recovery is the time between escalated behavior and an individual's return to baseline. Individuals need recovery anytime they escalate past the "triggered" phase of the stress response cycle, as their neurology has shifted toward fight or flight and needs time to reset, allowing the "thinking brain" to come back online. Interacting with an individual who has not fully recovered from escalated emotional states will most likely send them back into escalation.

Recovery often takes a lot of time and patience. The rules of responding to crisis also apply to recovery: no mouth, no eyes, no body. Supporting recovery means waiting until baseline behavior is present again. This can be tricky because we are often still escalated ourselves and our judgement of other's emotional state is impaired. We must check the behavior and ask ourselves, "is this typical baseline behavior?" Does this person usually present themselves as this compliant, this tired or this subdued?" If the answer is no, then continue to disengage until baseline behavior returns.

Return to Baseline

Return to Baseline

Although we have already discussed what a return to baseline looks like during the previous section, it is an important stage to revisit as it tends to be an area that challenges people and erodes the predictability and consistency at a critical stage of the process. In order to offer a healing environment, we must allow individuals to attain a full recovery back to emotional baseline before we re-engage with them.

A rule of thumb to assess for baseline is to wait until there are signs of boredom in the individual and they begin to approach you in an attempt to move on. When they do, check their behavior against what their typical baseline behavior looks like to make sure that they have recovered. Often you can "test" this by responding to an individual in a way that elicits a simple verbal or gestural response and assess that response to see if it matches baseline behavior. If not, return to the rules of disengagement – no mouth, no eyes, no body – and allow for continued recovery time.

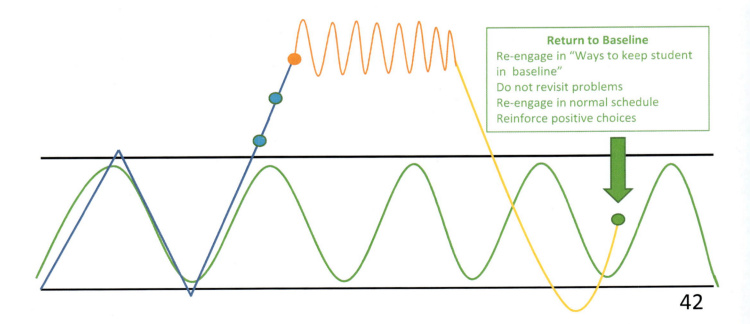

Return to Baseline
Re-engage in "Ways to keep student in baseline"
Do not revisit problems
Re-engage in normal schedule
Reinforce positive choices

Review

Allowing an individual to return to baseline before placing demands on them is mandatory for providing the type of predictable and consistent environment that promotes healing. Individuals must be able to recognize, over time, that no matter how bad things get, they have the time and space to recover before moving on. Once this pattern is established, recognized and begins to be trusted, tolerance will build and frequency, intensity and duration of escalation diminish.

Final Commentary

Holding true to this process will build trust and relationship over time as the person repeatedly encounters the same supportive interaction at the same points of escalation time and time again, and is consistently allowed the time and space they need to recover fully before being asked to move on. Additionally, the predictability and consistency that this process provides eliminates the anxiety around "what to do next?" when caring for emotionally charged individuals, allowing care providers to combat their own stress response and be more relaxed and confident in the face of challenging behavior.

We are playing a "long game." Although the intervention strategies covered in this book are the most effective way to reduce the likelihood of escalation and minimize the intensity and duration of behavior in the moment, it is the consistent repetition of these responses over time that rewires the brain and promotes self-regulation and healing.

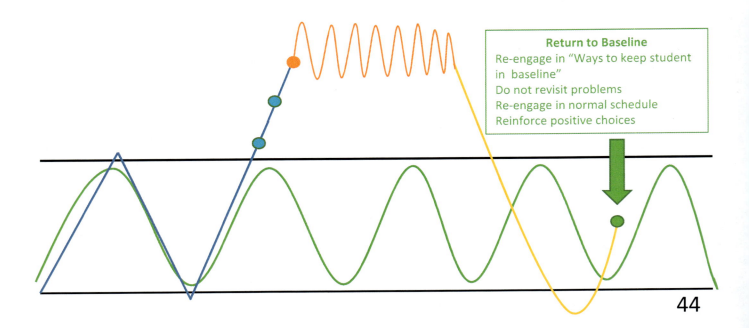

Return to Baseline
Re-engage in "Ways to keep student in baseline"
Do not revisit problems
Re-engage in normal schedule
Reinforce positive choices

Summary Overview

So often when we engage with escalated individuals, we tend to further their escalation rather than help resolve the situation, making it worse for ourselves, and the individuals we are trying to help. Understanding when to interact, at what level of intensity to engage, when to disengage all together, and when to re-engage after an escalation, not only helps the present situation, but supports reducing frequency, intensity and duration of escalation and crisis over time.

Emotions and brain function go hand in hand. When our emotions move us out of our baseline, our cognition begins to suffer and poor decision making follows. Being able to recognize the different stages of the stress response cycle, and knowing what intervention strategies match the needs of the brain at each phase of escalation, is how we avoid making things worse and begin to promote self-regulation and healing.

Baseline: emotions are stable; new learning can happen; negotiation is a valid option; understanding of "actions now effect outcomes later" is intact; tolerance is building.

Triggered: emotions are activated; brain is responding to signals that something is off and needs to be adjusted; cognition is still intact, but interaction is fragile as our neurology is seeking emotional stabilization and actively searching to fix what is beginning to impinge on us.

Escalation: our cognition is greatly compromised; emotions are driving our neurology; we are seeking "now" solutions as future consequences for present actions no longer register in the brain; peers and support providers are effected and often pulled into their own escalation at this stage. Carefully structured minimal communication of clear boundaries and total disengagement are mandatory; prolonged engagement, repeated demands and netotiation will only serve to escalate the situation.

Crisis: there is no logic here; zero understanding of present actions effecting future outcome; support providers are very likely to be escalated and suffering from poor cognition resulting in a mismatch of intervention; disengagement is mandatory

Recovery: both support providers and individuals need to go through this process; non-engagement is mandatory until individuals return to baseline (with the only rare exception being co-regulation in which careful planning and execution is a must).

References

Harris, N. B. (2015) *How Childhood Trauma Affects Health Across a Lifetime* [Video File]. Retrieved from https://www.youtube.com/watch?v=95ovIJ3dsNk

Perry, B. D. (2013) *Seven Slide Series: The Human Brain* [Video File]. Retrieved from https://www.youtube.com/watch?v=uOsgDkeH52o&t=2s

Perry, B. D. (2013) *Seven Slide Series: State-dependent Functioning* [Video File]. Retrieved from https://www.youtube.com/watch?v=1uCn7VX6BPQ&t=2s

Perry, B. D. (2013) *Seven Slide Series: Sensitization and Tolerance* [Video File]. Retrieved from https://www.youtube.com/watch?v=qv8dRfgZXV4

Perry, B. D. (2013) *Seven Slide Series: Threat Response Patterns* [Video File]. Retrieved from https://www.youtube.com/watch?v=sr-OXkk3i8E

Resources

For products, training, coaching and consultation services visit the website at: thevirtualbehaviorist.com

To go directly to videos about addressing behavior discussing real life examples, visit the YouTube channel at: TheVirtualBehaviorist.com

STRESS RESPONSE CONTINUUM WORKSHEET©

Created by: Josh Kuersten

Emotional Baseline
Looks Like:

First Signs Out of Baseline
Looks Like:
1.
2.
3.

Escalated
Looks Like:
1.
2.
3.

Crisis
Looks Like:

Crisis
No Mouth - No Eyes - No Body

Sympathetic Responses
1.
2.
3.

3+1 (Limit Setting)
1.
2.
3.
+ 1.

Recovery
No Mouth
No Eyes
No Body
Exception to the rule: Teach self-soothing (Co-Regulation)

Ways to keep student in Baseline

Return to Baseline
Re-engage in "Ways to keep student in baseline"
Do not revisit problems
Re-engage in normal schedule
Reinforce positive choices

Made in the USA
Monee, IL
15 November 2024

70220962R00031